# Guidelines for Library Services for People with Mental Retardation

Standards Committee Subcommittee to Develop
Guidelines for Library Services for People with Mental Retardation

Association of Specialized and Cooperative Library Agencies
American Library Association
Chicago 1999

Published by the Association of Specialized and Cooperative Library Agencies
American Library Association
50 East Huron Street
Chicago, IL 60611

ISBN 0-8389-8000-7

The paper used in this publication meets the minimum requirements of American National Standard for Information Sciences–Permanence of Paper for Printed Library Materials. ANSI 239.4-1992.

Printed in the United States of America.

# Contents

# Foreword

The *Guidelines for Library Services for People with Mental Retardation* is the result of the work of these members of the ASCLA Subcommittee to Develop Guidelines for Library Services for People with Mental Retardation:

Marilyn M. Irwin
Bloomington, IN

Elizabeth Ridler
Brooklyn, NY

Margaret L. Kirkpatrick
Wichita, KS

Marilyn Karrenbrock Stauffer
Tampa, FL

Dennis A. Norlin
Evanston, IL

Linda Lucas Walling
Columbia, SC

Ruth E. O'Donnell
Tallahassee, FL

Stewart L. Wells
Snow Hill, MD

The following individuals served on the Advisory Group:

Darrell L. Batson
Frederick, MD

Coy K. Hunsucker
Cincinnati, OH

Nancy Bolin
Columbia, MD

Bruce LaFleur
Columbia, SC

R. Brantley Cagle, Jr.
Lake Charles, LA

Rhea J. Rubin
Oakland, CA

Olga Green
Tallahassee, FL

# Introduction

## Context

Due to a number of factors, many libraries have neglected the needs of people with mental retardation. A primary factor is misunderstanding about the population as a whole. Assumptions are made that people who are mentally retarded live primarily in residential institutions; therefore, they do not reside within library service areas. Many consider people with mental retardation as nonreaders who would not use library resources. Furthermore, limited exposure to people who are mentally retarded may result in fear of the unknown causing further difficulty with the development of appropriate library services. *Guidelines for Library Services for People with Mental Retardation* has been developed to assist all libraries including school, public, academic, and specialized libraries such as prison and institutional libraries to better serve the needs of people of all ages who are mentally retarded.

Within that context, the following philosophy, values, and guiding principles were developed as a way of thinking.

### Philosophy
Libraries meet the needs of individuals who have mental retardation by determining and providing needed support to enable such individuals to successfully use, and receive the benefit of, available library services.

### Values
- Individuals with mental retardation are full, participating, contributing members of their communities—at school, at work, at home, and in recreational settings.

- Individuals with mental retardation are afforded dignity and respect through daily interactions, program decisions, and language use.

- Individuals with mental retardation are active and well-informed partners in decisions which affect their lives.

- Individuals with mental retardation and their families are involved in the design, operation, and monitoring of services and supports.

1

- All community members, those with and without mental retardation, must have information and skills to support the full and active participation of people who have mental retardation.

### Guiding Principles

- The library service needs of people with mental retardation cross the lifespan and the life areas.

- Library services promote inclusion and empowerment of people with mental retardation.

- Library services maximize access to information for people with mental retardation and their families.

## Status of "Standards"

*Standards for Libraries at Institutions for the Mentally Retarded* was published by the Association of Specialized and Cooperative Library Agencies (ASCLA) of the American Library Association (ALA) in 1981 as the first ALA standards document to address the needs of people with mental retardation. Prior to these standards, the ALA participated in the development of the *Accreditation Manual for Hospitals* (JCAH 1971) published by the Joint Commission on Accreditation of Hospitals. Until the present guidelines were developed, these were the only standards specifically related to library services for people with mental retardation with which the American Library Association had been involved. Both of these works addressed only the libraries within institutional settings.

In 1992, Ruth O'Donnell surveyed state libraries across the United States to determine whether standards or guidelines for library services for people with mental retardation had been developed at the state level. *Library Services for Persons who are Mentally Retarded* (Florida Department of State 1987), published by the State Library of Florida, was the only such document to emerge from that survey.

Due to the age of the first set of *Standards*, the increasing presence of people who are mentally retarded within the community, a lack of material to guide libraries as they attempt to serve the population, and a limited understanding of the library and information needs of people with mental retardation and their families, ASCLA appointed a committee to revise the 1981 *Standards*. The following document is the outcome of that decision.

## Procedure to Develop Guidelines

Several steps were taken to bring *Guidelines for Library Services for People with Mental Retardation* forward. These included:

1. The charge was given by the ASCLA Standards Committee to revise "Standards for Libraries at Institutions for the Mentally Retarded" in June 1992.

2. The Subcommittee was officially appointed in June 1992, and meetings were held at most Annual and Midwinter conferences beginning in June 1992. Issues discussed at the meetings included:

   **AUDIENCE**: A document for all libraries is needed, not just for institution libraries; however, there is value in updating the standards for those few libraries at institutions that remain. Discussion at that point was about whether the Subcommittee should develop one document for institutions and a second for all libraries, and whether the latter should be "Standards" or "Guidelines." The ASCLA Standards Review Committee clarified that the primary responsibility of the Subcommittee was to develop a document to serve all libraries, and they approved changing the name of the Subcommittee and that of the document to "Guidelines for Library Services for People with Mental Retardation." Because the number of institutions serving people with mental retardation that have libraries has dropped to less than 100, the Committee did not feel a separate document for institutions would have a broad enough market to warrant development.

   **DEFINITION:** After significant discussion, the Subcommittee decided not to use the broader designation "developmental disabilities," but to focus instead on mental retardation. The definition of mental retardation adopted by the American Association on Mental Retardation was accepted for use by the Subcommittee and the Standards Review Committee.

   **INCLUSION OF ADA**: The Subcommittee and Committee approved the approach that the Americans with Disabilities Act will be covered in the legislative history section, but a lot of detail will not be provided because that information is available in other publications.

   **SURVEY OF STATE LIBRARIES**: In Spring 1992, Ruth O'Donnell conducted a survey of state library agencies to determine whether state standards or guidelines were available. Florida has the only guidelines that could be identified.

   **ADVISORY COMMITTEE AND FIELD REVIEWERS**: An Advisory Committee was appointed by the ASCLA Standards Committee. A list of field reviewers was put together. In July 1997, the draft document was submitted to the Advisory Committee and to the field reviewers.

   **FUNDING FOR THE WORK OF THE COMMITTEE**: Funding support for the development of the *Guidelines* came from the State Library of Florida and the Institute for the Study of Developmental Disabilities at Indiana University.

# Overview

## Definitions

The definition used to define mental retardation is the one adopted by the American Association on Mental Retardation (1992).

*Mental retardation* refers to substantial limitations in present functioning. It is characterized by significantly subaverage intellectual functioning, existing concurrently with related limitations in two or more of the following applicable adaptive skill areas: communication, self-care, home living, social skills, community use, self-direction, health and safety, functional academics, leisure, and work. Mental retardation manifests before age 18.

The following four assumptions are essential to the application of the definition:

1.  Valid assessment considers cultural and linguistic diversity as well as differences in communication and behavioral factors;

2.  The existence of limitations in adaptive skills occurs within the context of community environments typical of the individual's age peers and is indexed to the person's individualized needs for supports;

3.  Specific adaptive limitations often coexist with strengths in other adaptive skills or other personal capabilities; and

4.  With appropriate supports over a sustained period, the life functioning of the person with mental retardation will generally improve. (p. 5)

## Historical Overview

It is difficult to plan for tomorrow without realizing how people with mental retardation arrived at where they are today. This overview will therefore provide an historical context for the *Guidelines.*

Prior to 1800, few services were available for people with mental retardation other than those provided by families and churches. The first half of the 19th century saw a flurry of activities by individuals who took an interest in the educational, behavioral, and residential needs of people with mental retardation. Many of the initiatives proposed and implemented were well intended, but began to pull people with more severe disabilities out of community settings and move them into segregated environments. It was during the early 1840s, for example, that Dorothea Dix advocated development of specialized residential facilities to improve treatment. Her crusade focused on the mistreatment of people with mental retardation, but it is also thought to have initiated the move toward institutionalization of people with more significant disabilities. The original intent for institutions was to provide training that would enable people with mental retardation to move back into their home communities; however, people began to realize by the early 20th century that, although skills could be taught, there was little chance for a "cure". Institutions then shifted from having a training role to having a custodial care role for people with severe disabilities.

The latter half of the 20th century has seen significant changes in treatment, services, and legislation supporting the needs of people with mental retardation, much of which was brought about through the advocacy of families of people who are disabled. In 1950, the Association for Retarded Citizens (currently The Arc) was established, primarily by parents, to coordinate advocacy efforts on behalf of people with mental retardation. Also in 1950, Aid to the Permanently and Totally Disabled (APTD) was added to Social Security to provide assistance to some qualified individuals with mental retardation. This program existed until 1972 when it was expanded by the Supplemental Security Income (SSI) Program.

One of the leading family members advocating services for people with mental retardation was President John F. Kennedy, who had a sister with mental retardation. In 1961, he established the President's Panel on Mental Retardation. Many of the 95 recommendations of this Panel set the agenda for federal programs in the area of mental retardation for the years that followed. The Mental Retardation Facilities and Community Mental Health Centers Construction Act (PL 88-164) was one outcome of the work of the Panel. This law and its subsequent reauthorizations and amendments as the Developmental Disabilities Assistance and Bill of Rights Acts (PL 91-517, PL 94-103, PL 95-602, PL 97-35, PL 98-527, PL 100-146, and PL 104-183) have included the following key concepts and provisions:

- rights to appropriate treatment and services
- due process safeguards
- services governed by Individual Habilitation Plans (IHPs)
- establishment of Developmental Disabilities Councils for planning and coordination in each state
- establishment of university affiliated programs (UAPs) for interdisciplinary training, technical assistance, research, and dissemination
- establishment of a Protection and Advocacy System in each state
- an emphasis on "independence, productivity, and integration in the community" as goals and outcomes for people with mental retardation

These initiatives have cleared the way for the reduced population in, and closing of, a significant number of large state institutions across the country. People with mental retardation are now living in communities. Some live in nursing and group homes, and an increasing number live in their own apartments, trailers, condominiums, and houses with the support of others in semi independent living arrangements.

Among other efforts, members of The Arc and other advocacy groups worked at the grass roots level to establish educational programs for their children. Although many states had enacted state legislation supporting educational programs for children who were disabled, students with more severe disabilities were not universally served until passage of the Education for All Handicapped Children Act of 1975 (PL 94-142). Public Law 94-142 and its subsequent reauthorizations and amendments as the Individuals with Disabilities Education Act (IDEA) (PL 98-199, PL 99-457, PL 100-630, PL 101-476, PL 102-56, PL 102-119, and 105-17) mandate free, appropriate public education for all children with disabilities. Prior to passage of this landmark legislation, parents often paid for private programs or established their own under the Arc umbrella so their children could receive an education. Additional key components and provisions of IDEA include

- education in the least restrictive environment provision of special education and related services (speech therapy, transportation, assistive technology, etc.) that provide educational benefit
- services outlined in Individualized Education Plans (IEPs)
- due process safeguards for parents
- multi-source evaluations
- early intervention and preschool programs for eligible children from birth
- planning for transition from school to adult life outlined in Individualized Transition Plans (ITPs)

The Rehabilitation Act of 1973 (PL 93-112) and its reauthorizations and amendments (PL 95-602 and PL 99-506) provide numerous employment related provisions that impact on the lives of people with mental retardation. These include:

- funding for vocational evaluations, training, placement, job-related counseling, and follow along
- services outlined in Individualized Written Rehabilitation Plans (IWRPs)
- the priority to serve people with the most severe disabilities
- supported employment in the community

Public Law 93-112 also included a provision that states:
"No otherwise qualified handicapped individual...shall solely by reason of his handicap, be excluded from the participation in, be denied the benefits of, or be subjected to discrimination under any program or activity receiving federal financial assistance..."

The civil rights mandates found in the Rehabilitation Act were expanded in the Americans with Disabilities Act (ADA) of 1990. The ADA and Rehabilitation Act prohibit discrimination against people with disabilities on the part of all entities, public and private, in employment and access to services. Specific provisions of the Americans with Disabilities Act that impact on the lives of people with mental retardation include:

- employment opportunities with "reasonable accommodations" made by employers to

meet the needs of employees with a broad range of disabilities
- prohibition of discrimination by state and local government and public entities in services, programs, and activities, including those provided by state, public, academic, and school libraries not covered under the Rehabilitation Act
- prohibition of discrimination in public accommodations and services provided by private entities, including privately operated museums and archive collections that are open to the public
- access to telecommunications relay services

Taken as a whole, the legislation of the last 40 years has made a significant impact on the lives of people with disabilities; however, current work in the field indicates that people with mental retardation may be in the community, but they are rarely considered part of the community. Children with mental retardation may be educated in buildings with their peers, but many are bussed to schools other than the ones attended by their siblings and neighbors. In most educational settings, they are given few opportunities to interact with their peers. Decisions are often made for children and adults with mental retardation by others, including basic issues such as where and with whom they live, where they go for recreation, and what type of employment they have. For many, this means they do not know how to make choices for themselves.

## Current Trends

Many of the current initiatives are moving toward increased community membership for people with mental retardation with the concept of full participation in school, work, home, and recreational environments. In order to achieve this, people with mental retardation must become empowered to be their own self advocates and systems must change to support that goal.

In schools, students with mental retardation are being given increasing opportunities to receive their education in neighborhood schools and in classrooms with their nondisabled peers. In order to meet their needs in the inclusive classroom, the curriculum and instruction are being adapted and supports are provided, if needed.

Community-based jobs are being found every day for individuals with mental retardation, and many employers have indicated overall satisfaction with the output of this new workforce. Programs like the National Home of Your Own Project help individuals live in community residential environments of their choosing. State and federal funding is in place to support employment and independent living, but those same funding streams are not uniformly available from state to state causing some to be left out of the programs. Furthermore, successful employment and independent living may result in the elimination of other safety net programs, such as Medicaid and Medicare to meet health care needs, creating significant disincentives to participation.

Many community-based recreation programs are making efforts to meet the needs of people with mental retardation, but staff members rarely have adequate training to provide appropriate services. Transportation to these programs is also often a problem. Other programs, such as Very Special Arts and Special Olympics, exist to fill the gap, but they continue to segregate people with mental retardation. One handicap often experienced by people with mental retardation is a lack of friends and profound loneliness.

# Service Needs of People with Mental Retardation

## Introduction

People with mental retardation use the library for the same purposes as other library users. Their interests are generally similar to the interests of their age-mates. They come to the library seeking information, recreation, instruction, and inspiration. They can become enthusiastic, effective, responsible library users. Many are fond of books and computers and enjoy storytelling, read-alouds, movies, magazines, and music. Their abilities are usually less recognized than their disabilities, but they have both. Their disabilities require modifications of services and collections as well as of the facility itself if they are to be full participants in the library's programs. Modifications should build on their abilities and strengths.

For any individual, mental retardation is likely to be only one of a cluster of disabilities. Mental retardation may be either the primary or a secondary disability. This section introduces typical functional disabilities which are sometimes associated with mental retardation and describes adaptations which focus on ability and which can make programs and services accessible.

## Functional Disabilities

### Cognition and perception

Impairment of the ability to learn (i.e., cognition) is the most familiar feature of mental retardation. Impairment of cognition in mental retardation is generalized, but the individual can still learn if certain conditions are met. Individuals with mental retardation may also experience impairment of their ability to correctly interpret and use information they receive through the senses (i.e., perception). Perceptual impairment is usually specific. For example, the person may have great difficulty using visual information but may learn well through the tactile-kinesthetic mode. Reading is a common problem for people with cognitive and perceptual disabilities. In general, complex interior decoration and complicated floor plans are confusing for people with both functional impairments.

**GUIDELINES:**
The library provides interesting, age-appropriate fiction and nonfiction materials at low reading levels. Materials are available which communicate information through different senses (e.g., tangibles, large print, picture books, high interest/low vocabulary, adult basic education, video, audio). Adaptive computer software and hardware are provided. The facility is planned with attention to the need to avoid complex, complicated floor plans and color schemes.

## *Communication*

Many people with mental retardation have difficulty understanding verbal and written communications and they have difficulty sending messages that are understood by others. Some have severe hearing and/or visual impairments. Many use spoken language to communicate. Others communicate through adaptive communication devices that use visual, auditory, or tactile symbols. Many use sign language. Some communicate through their behavior. It is safe to say that every individual has developed a system of communication, but not all communication systems are easily understood.

**GUIDELINES:**
Library staff members are prepared to discover and use a communication system that meets the needs of the individual for both expressive and receptive communication.

## *Behavior*

The most observable aspects of mental retardation are often emotional and social in nature. Among the behaviors which are sometimes, but not always, associated with mental retardation are inattention, hyperactivity, impulsivity, a strong desire for control, demands for attention, disruptions, antisocial behavior, inability to respond to human interaction or–conversely–a strong need for human interaction, fascination with objects, stereotyped behavior, self-stimulating behaviors, and self-destructive behaviors. Some individuals can interact with other people only to a limited degree, some have only minimal social skills, and some are frightened by the unpredictability of human behavior. Some have a strong need for sameness and a hypersensitivity to touch. Some are highly emotional. Some have involuntary tics, obsessive thoughts, irritability, anxiety, mood swings, and/or behavior changes.

**GUIDELINES:**
Library staff members recognize that some people cannot control their own behavior. They recognize that a fear of the unknown may be the origin of bizarre behavior, and they understand that for many individuals, behavior is a means of communication. Staff members seek to understand the meaning of unusual behaviors and are prepared to tolerate a wide range of behaviors. They are prepared to help other people learn greater tolerance for unusual behaviors as well.

## Motor functions

Many people with mental retardation have difficulty with standing and/or walking as well as with using their fingers and hands. Motor impairments to the organs of speech may make it difficult to speak clearly.

**GUIDELINES:**
The library makes reasonable accommodations for wheelchairs and other mobility devices. Door handles, water faucets, and other devices and equipment which must be manipulated are adapted for people who cannot use their hands.

## Chronic health conditions

Chronic health conditions such as congenital heart defects, seizures, respiratory problems, and immune deficiencies sometimes accompany mental retardation. Some individuals have technologically sophisticated devices that support their lives.

**GUIDELINES:**
Library staff members are prepared to accommodate the individual needs of people with chronic health conditions. They are prepared to respond appropriately to health emergencies.

## Multiple disabilities

As this Section makes clear, it is common for people with mental retardation to have other disabilities as well. The effects of multiple disabilities are exponential because the disabilities interact to make learning and other life activities more difficult.

**GUIDELINES:**
Library staff members are prepared to work with people individually to discover their strongest communication mode, their level of understanding, and their information need in any given situation.

# Access to Programs and Services

## Planning for services

People with mental retardation usually require modifications if they are to use libraries successfully.

**GUIDELINES:**
The library promotes its services to people with mental retardation in its community. There is an advisory committee among whose members are people with mental

retardation and their advocates. There is careful consideration of the most effective method or combination of methods for providing services to people with mental retardation in the community (i.e., inclusion, special needs center, outreach). The library encourages families and service providers to work with the library in making services available for people with mental retardation. A designated library staff member coordinates and supervises services for people with mental retardation, but collections, services, and programs are adapted for the anticipated needs of people with mental retardation and carried out by all library staff. Appropriate adaptive technology is provided. The library's public relations activities and publicity include modifications for people with mental retardation. The library's evaluation component includes evaluation of services for people with mental retardation, their families, the professionals who work with them, and other advocates.

## *Getting around in the facility*

Individuals with mental retardation need directional signs and signals that communicate in ways they can understand; they need barrier-free access to the library facility and within it. They need attention to issues of safety and security.

**GUIDELINES:**
Directional signs are large with simple, clear messages. They are placed where they are highly visible. Universal or other easily recognized symbols are used along with the directional signs. Auditory, visual, and tactile symbols and signals support communication.

The facility is barrier-free to wheelchairs and other mobility devices, and door handles and other devices are designed for easy manipulation. Barrier-free routes are clearly marked. The floor plan, color scheme, and interior decoration take into account the individual's need for a facility with minimal confusion.

Fire alarms and other emergency alert signals have both auditory and visual components. Such components take into account the visual and auditory frequencies most likely to trigger seizures. The library has a plan, developed with the assistance of the advisory committee, for safely evacuating people with mental retardation from the building in case of an emergency.

## *Interactions with library staff*

People with mental retardation, like all library patrons, need positive interactions in which they are treated with respect and through which they satisfy their need for information, whether that need is for a book to read or hear or for an answer to a question. Individuals with mental retardation may also need extra time and guidance to make decisions about and utilize appropriate library services.

**GUIDELINES:**
Library staff members see all library patrons as people of ability, worthy of assistance. Library staff receive ongoing training to meet the changing needs of people with mental retardation. Staff members establish effective communication so that they can understand the information need, and they assure that the information need is satisfied. Library staff allow sufficient time for decision making and utilization of library services. They provide appropriate guidance when needed. They model appropriate interaction for other staff members and other library patrons.

## Locating and retrieving library materials

Some people with mental retardation have had little involvement with books and other materials. Many have had little opportunity to learn to choose books, toys, or other materials based on their own interests. Because reading is a common problem and because library catalogs (both print and electronic) generally require reading, people with mental retardation may need assistance in identifying the materials which will satisfy their information need. Those who have difficulty using their hands may need assistance, such as turning catalog cards or keying in commands.

Difficulty with reading also makes locating an item in the library stacks difficult because most call numbers or location symbols require reading. Stacks with their rows upon rows of books can be disorienting. Wheelchairs and other mobility devices are difficult to maneuver in narrow spaces. Books can be difficult to pull from the shelves if individuals are in wheelchairs or if they have difficulty using their hands.

**GUIDELINES:**
Library staff members take time to help the patron with mental retardation choose materials according to his or her interests. Library staff members willingly help people with mental retardation understand and use the catalog and other tools to identify and retrieve the materials that satisfy the information need. Library staff locate and retrieve materials when needed.

## Using materials and services

People with mental retardation, like other library patrons, may have little understanding of common library policies, and they may not understand how to care for library materials. Many have not had opportunities to develop the social skills that could help them be more accepted in society. Some need adapted policies or services.

**GUIDELINES:**
Library staff members explain library policies and are prepared to modify them if necessary to meet individual needs. Adaptive devices and equipment are provided as they are needed. Care of library materials is demonstrated and explained in ways that can be understood by the individual. Library instruction is appropriately modified. Library programs are adapted for the enjoyment and pleasure of people with mental retardation,

including adapted communication and the use of multiple formats. When planning programs or other activities, library staff members build in opportunities for people with mental retardation to interact with each other and with people who are not mentally retarded. Opportunities are provided for learning and practicing social skills. Appropriate interactions are modeled for both individuals with mental retardation and other library patrons.

## Summary

People with mental retardation have information needs that the library can meet, and they have the potential to become effective library users. In addition to generalized problems with learning (i.e., cognition), individuals may have difficulty with perception, communication, behavior, motor functions, and/or chronic health conditions. Because multiple disabilities are common, people with mental retardation need modifications of the collection, the facilities, and the services. The library's planning process incorporates modifications to the collection such as interesting, age-appropriate materials in many formats that communicate information through different senses. Appropriate adaptive technology is provided. The facility is barrier-free and planned to avoid complex, complicated floor plans and color schemes. Directional signs are highly visible with simple, clear messages accompanied by easily recognized symbols. Auditory, visual, and tactile symbols are provided.

Because individuals with mental retardation use various communication systems, library staff members are prepared to discover and use a communication system that meets the needs of the individual. Library staff members are prepared to work with people individually to discover their strongest communication mode, their level of understanding, and their information need in any given situation. They establish effective communication so that they can understand the information need, and they assure that the information need is satisfied. They model appropriate interaction for other staff members and other library patrons.

Library staff members take time to help the patron with mental retardation choose materials according to his or her interests and willingly help people with mental retardation identify and retrieve the materials they want. Library policies are modified as appropriate to meet an individual's need. Library instruction and library programs are also appropriately modified.

# Needs for Information about Mental Retardation

With increasing integration of people with mental retardation in the community, the need for information about mental retardation also increases. Family members of the individuals are one group with information needs. Parents in general have very little knowledge of the needs of their children at birth, yet needed information is often available to them from sources as close as the parent next door or around the corner. Parents and other guardians of children with mental retardation also have little knowledge to meet the needs of their children; however, because of the complexity and low incidence of the disability, the sources to meet their information needs are not as close or as obvious.

Moore, Morton, and Southard (1984), parents of children with disabilities, wrote: "Raising a child who is handicapped requires more knowledge and understanding—of the child, of oneself, and of others—than is required in raising a child who is not handicapped" (p. 17). Furthermore, Mayfield-Smith et al. (1990) found in their national study that 84 percent of the consumers defined as people with developmental disabilities (which includes mental retardation) and their families needed information on disability-related services within the previous six months. Additionally, they found that 78.6 percent said they needed that kind of information at least monthly (p. 9).

Information needs include resources to help family members understand the disability itself. Family members also need to have information for decision making in areas such as early intervention services, the benefit of specialized therapies, special education programming, employment and residential options, and estate and guardianship planning. Information in the form of referrals can also help parents and other caregivers locate appropriate services such as accessible dentists, agencies that provide respite services, and lawyers with disability expertise.

Other family members and caregivers also need information. Grandparents, aunts, and uncles frequently provide support for the parents and the individual with the disability, and they often seek information to improve their understanding. With the attention given to the child with mental retardation, siblings frequently feel left out, ignored, and confused. An increasing number of quality children's materials are being developed to help young children understand the needs of a sibling who has mental retardation. As the children grow into adulthood and the parents age and die, siblings often take on increasing responsibility for the support of the person with mental retardation making it all the more important that siblings understand the needs of their brothers and sisters.

With increasing integration of people with mental retardation in school, work, recreation, and other community environments, there is a greater need for understanding by the general population. Family physicians, for example, rarely have specialized training to meet the needs of people with mental retardation, yet parents want their children to go to the same doctor as the rest of the family. Teachers need to understand the educational implications of the many rare syndromes and disorders associated with mental retardation. Employers can more easily make adaptations if they are knowledgeable about the disability. Recreation specialists can better determine the likes and dislikes of the individual if they understand the disability.

In summary, current and accurate information about mental retardation can serve a wide audience, and should be included in school, public, and academic libraries.

# Service Outcomes

## Definition of Service Outcomes for People with Mental Retardation

As increasing numbers of individuals with mental retardation remain with their families or live and work in their own neighborhoods, libraries become an affordable information and recreation outlet within the community. The individual with mental retardation may visit the library independently or with family and friends, and he or she would have personal outcomes in mind for the visit. Some individuals who are clients of agencies have a written individualized program. The library may work with the agency to meet the goals of the individualized program, but those goals must be understood as the goals of the agency, not necessarily the goals of the individual. All individuals derive value from the services of the library. Evaluating the service based on service outcomes means that the library considers the extent to which the individuals served have attained their personal goals and objectives related to the library. Service outcomes are based on individual choice and decision-making.

The library should also consider the extent to which it (the library) has attained its goals. Thus, there are three basic questions: What did the service do for the person? Were the goals and objectives established by the library attained? Do the library's mission statement and service outcomes meet the service needs of individuals with mental retardation?

## Context

In order to evaluate a service based on service outcomes, the library must discover the personal goals and objectives of the users of the services through an appropriate mechanism. Individual library users with mental retardation must be interviewed or surveyed directly rather than through an intermediary. Interviews and surveys must be adapted to the communication mode the individual uses. Norlin (1995) gives suggestions for interviewing adults with mental retardation. He makes it clear that adults can speak for themselves if the interviewer takes certain factors into account.

# Service Outcomes for the Individual with Mental Retardation

The Accreditation Council on Services for People with Disabilities has established service outcomes for individuals and service providers that can be applied in any setting. The following outcomes, which are directly applicable in libraries, are adapted from those developed by the Accreditation Council (1993):

**1. Individuals choose personal goals**: The individual understands that the library is an option that he or she can use to pursue personal goals.

**2. Individuals have access to the facility**: The library has designed and initiated a process to enable all individuals to use the facility effectively.

**3. Individuals help design and have access to the services of the library they choose**: The library includes individuals in the planning process and provides needed support and assistance on choosing and using desired services.

**4. The individual can use the library and its services for the purposes and with the frequency desired**: The library has designed and initiated a process that enables the person to participate fully in the services of the library.

**5. The individual has opportunities to choose to interact with other members of the community**: The library provides accessible opportunities for interaction.

**6. The individual can exercise his/her rights to equal access to the facility and its services and to appropriate types and formats of materials**: The facility is accessible, the collection includes appropriate types and formats of materials, and the staff is prepared to effectively assist individuals in achieving access.

**7. The individual is respected**: Library staff demonstrate respect for the person; staff interactions and service practices reflect concern for the person's opinions, feelings, and preferences.

**8. Confidentiality is respected**: The individual, not the library or another service agency, decides when to share personal information.

**9. The individual's support networks (e.g., family, advocates, service agency staff members) are adequately served by the library**: The library involves representatives of support groups in library planning and provides appropriate materials in a variety of formats.

**10. The individual experiences continuity and security**: The library provides for continuity and security in its facility and services.

**11. The individual is satisfied with the library's services**: There are appropriate and effective services offered to meet the individual's needs and expectations.

## Performance Measures for Library Services for People with Mental Retardation

**1. The library has a mission statement and desired outcomes that are clearly stated**: There is a strategic/long range plan that includes the needs of people with mental retardation and is regularly reviewed. This includes a financial commitment to fulfill the mission and desired outcomes.

**2. The library conducts ongoing evaluation of success in achieving desired outcomes:** The evaluation focuses on the people served, the program, and/or the organization and management of resources.

**3. The library includes input and involvement from people served and others in its evaluation and planning activities**: Individuals, family members, guardians, advocates, and staff participate, through committee meetings or written responses, in the collection and analysis of data to measure the accomplishment of objectives. Representatives of other agencies with which the library works and members of the larger community participate in the collection, analysis, and review of data to determine the accomplishment of outcomes and/or barriers to their accomplishment.

**4. The library implements a program for continuous quality enhancement**: The program examines, on a regular basis, the organization processes that contribute to outcomes. Employment, training, and education of staff are based on an analysis of programs and processes that must contribute to the achievement of consumer outcomes.

## Summary

A service outcomes approach to evaluation requires a focus on individual needs and choices. The library must be aware that people with mental retardation, like other library users, have individual wants, needs, and goals. They must be provided with an array of choices that are accessible. The library must plan to provide not only choices but also the support and assistance individuals require to achieve their goals. Individuals with mental retardation, their families, advocates, and service providers must be involved in planning, carrying out, and evaluating the library's service program.

# References Cited

The Accreditation Council on Services for People with Disabilities. 1993. *Outcome Based Performance Measures.* Landover, MD: Author.

American Association on Mental Retardation. 1992. *Mental Retardation: Definition, Classification, And Systems Of Supports,* 9th ed. Washington, DC: Author.

American Library Association, Association of Specialized and Cooperative Library Agencies. 1981. *Standards for Libraries at Institutions for the Mentally Retarded.* Chicago: American Library Association.

Florida Department of State, Division of Library and Information Services. 1987. *Library Services For Persons Who Are Mentally Retarded.* Tallahassee: Florida Department of State.

Joint Commission on Accreditation of Hospitals (JCAH). 1971. *Accreditation Manual for Hospitals.* Chicago: Joint Commission on Accreditation of Hospitals.

Mayfield-Smith, K., Yajnik, G. G., Toon, T. L., & Morse, R. 1990. *Study to Determine the Feasibility and Desirability of a Nationwide Information and Referral System for Persons with Developmental Disabilities: Executive Summary.* Columbia, SC: University of South Carolina, Center for Developmental Disabilities.

Moore, C., Morton, K. G., & Southard, A. 1984. A reader's guide for parents of children with mental, physical, or emotional disabilities. *Exceptional Parent,* 14(2), 16-17.

Norlin, D. 1995. Helping adults with mental retardation satisfy their information needs. In L. L. Walling and M. M. Irwin (Eds)., *Information Services for People with Developmental Disabilities: The library Manager's Handbook,* (181-195). Westport, CT: Greenwood Press.